DATE DUE

NOV 5 1993			
AUG 10 1994			

The Library Store   #47-0103

SKIN

Brian Ward

FRANKLIN WATTS

New York/London/Sydney/Toronto

© Franklin Watts 1990

Franklin Watts Inc
387 Park Avenue South
New York
NY 10016

Editor: Helen Broxholme
Design: K & Co
Consultant: Dr Philip Sawney

Illustrations: Aziz Khan

Photographs: Bubbles 4b, 12t, 14b, 26t, 28t; Colorsport 24c; Eye Ubiquitous 9tr; Chris
Fairclough 4t, 6t, 14t, 15 (all), 18b, 21tl, 21tr, 28b; Chris Fairclough Colour Library/
Mike Morton 23t; Mike Galletly 5t, 5br; Robert Harding Picture Library 12b, 22t, 24t,
25tr; Hutchison Library 20b; National Medical Slide Bank 18t, 23bl, 23br, 24br, 25bl;
Science Photo Library 6b, 10t, 11t, 16t, 16b, 17t, 17c, 19 (all), 20t, 21b, 25tl, 25br, 26bl,
26br, 27t, 29t; Frank Spooner Picture Library 22b; Supersport 9tl; John Watney 24bl;
ZEFA cover, 5bl, 8t, 8br, 25tc.

Library of Congress Cataloging-in-Publication Data
Ward, Brian.
    Skin / Brian Ward.
        p.   cm. — (Health guide)
    Summary: Discusses the functions, care, and properties of skin, as
well as the blemishes, allergies, and infections that can affect it.
    ISBN 0-531-14072-5
    1. Skin—Diseases—Juvenile literature.   [2. Skin—Juvenile
literature.   [1. Skin.]   I. Title.   II. Series.
    RL86.W37   1990
    612.7'9—dc20   90-31224
                                                        CIP AC

CONTENTS

FEELING GOOD

"Feeling good" is not just the absence of illness. We all have good days and bad days, and sometimes are so tired, we want nothing else but to go back to bed. But on the good days, you feel bouncy and ready to tackle anything.

What does this have to do with your skin? Your skin is an indicator of how you feel. If you stay up very late and don't get enough sleep, your skin will probably look pale, and the skin around your eyes will be puffy.

If you are ill, or are run-down, your skin suffers too. Skin problems like pimples and cold sores are more likely to appear if your resistance is weakened by some other condition. But when you feel fit, rested, and

▷ When you feel good, you look good as well. Exercise literally makes your skin glow, because it stimulates blood flow in the skin.

◁ Variations in human skin and hair color are due to differences in the amount of melanin pigment they contain. People who live in hot countries have darker skin and hair containing lots of melanin which protects them from strong sun. Those from cooler climates contain less melanin and have fair skin and hair.

on top of the world, your skin shows it too. Inner health means that your skin will be clear and will look good.

Because the skin is almost the only visible part of your body (apart from the cornea of the eye), it is easy to become oversensitive about your skin and to worry unnecessarily. Almost everyone has suffered from pimples in their 'teens, and they nearly always clear up as you get older.

Skin is very varied in appearance and texture. Some people have pale skin, while in others the skin is darkly pigmented. The skin also varies in thickness in different parts of the body, and is thickest where the body needs protection from rubbing.

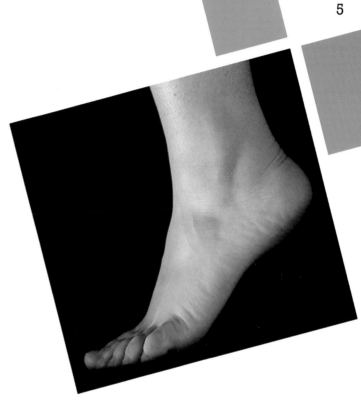

◁ As children, our skin is thin and flexible, but as we age, it hardens and creases.

△ The skin on the soles of our feet and the palms of our hands ▽ is very thick.

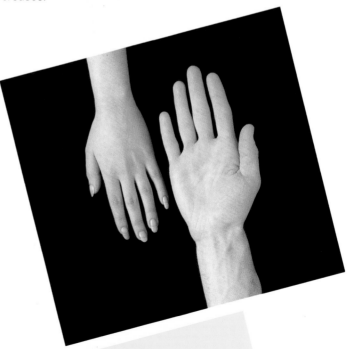

LOOKING AT SKIN

Skin is the largest organ of the body, and has many different functions. The most important is to protect the internal organs and structures of the body.

All of our living cells live in a watery environment of blood or other body fluids. The skin is the outer container which helps to maintain constant, watery conditions within the body. It consists of two main layers. The skin we can see is completely composed of dead cells, making up the outer layer or epidermis. These cells have separated from the dermis layer beneath, creating the epidermis. As living cells are constantly produced by the dermis they become filled with a tough material called keratin (nails and hair are made of keratin too). By the time these cells have reached the skin surface, they are dead and will eventually flake off to make way for new cells.

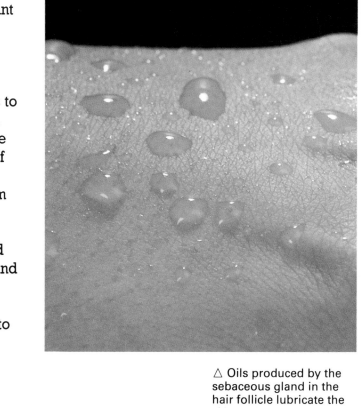

△ Oils produced by the sebaceous gland in the hair follicle lubricate the skin and make it waterproof. Water can leave the body as sweat, through the sweat glands, but it can't get in.

◁ This electron micrograph shows a section through the skin. On the surface are the large, scale-like epidermal cells, while underneath are the tightly packed cells of the dermis, containing collagen fibers and blood vessels. The flattened epidermal cells on the surface are dead, and contain tough keratin to strengthen them.

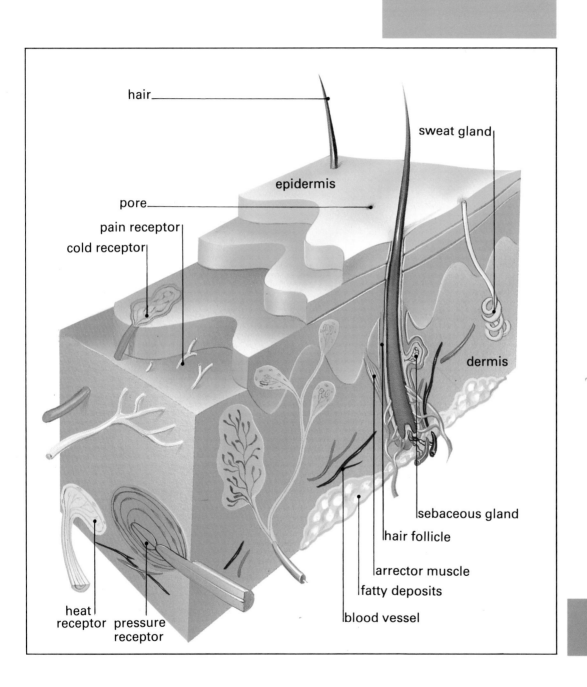

hair

sweat gland

epidermis

pore

pain receptor

cold receptor

dermis

heat receptor

pressure receptor

sebaceous gland

hair follicle

arrector muscle

fatty deposits

blood vessel

△ This diagram shows the major structures of the dermis and epidermis – the two main layers of the skin.

HOW SKIN WORKS

Running through the dermis are many tough, flexible fibers of collagen, which give the skin its strength and elasticity. As we age, the collagen reinforcing the skin becomes tougher, so the skin is less flexible and tends to form lines or wrinkles.

Small nerves in the dermis have endings which are sensitive to touch, pain, and temperature. These nerve endings are most common in areas like the fingertips and lips, which are important sensory areas. Sweat glands in the skin produce perspiration to cool the body, and these also remove some excess salt from the blood.

Most of the skin is covered with hair follicles, from which the hair grows. Glands in the follicles produce oily sebum that lubricates the skin and keeps the epidermis supple.

▽ The epidermal layer of the skin contains several different sensory receptors which detect either touch, pressure, pain or temperature. Each receptor can only detect one "feeling."

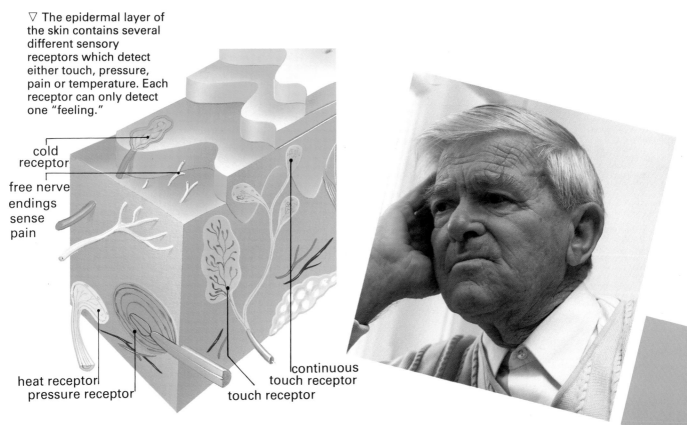

cold receptor

free nerve endings sense pain

heat receptor
pressure receptor

touch receptor

continuous touch receptor

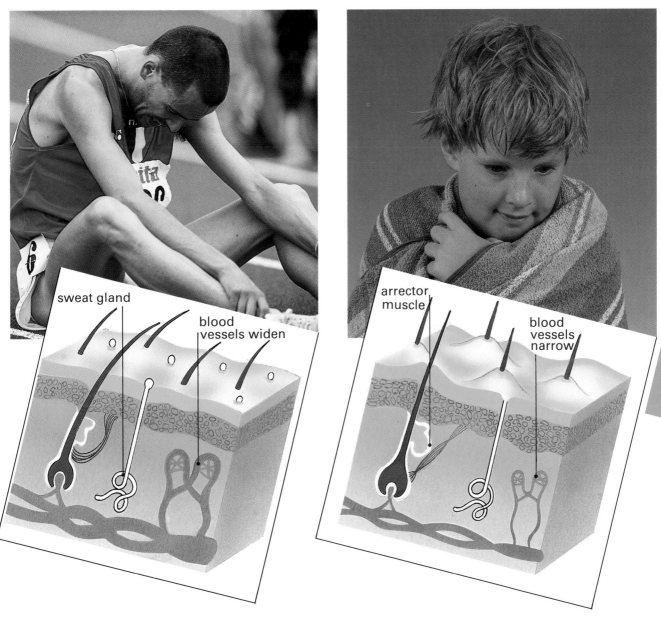

sweat gland

blood vessels widen

arrector muscle

blood vessels narrow

△ The human body works best at 98°F. The skin helps to keep this temperature constant.

When we are hot, our bodies need to lose heat. The skin does this in two ways. Blood vessels in the skin widen allowing more heat from the blood to escape. Sweat, produced by the seat glands, takes heat away from the skin as it evaporates.

△ When we are cold, our skin tries to stop heat escaping. The blood vessels in the skin become narrow, reducing the amount of heat lost and making the skin look pale. The arrector muscles of of the hair follicle pull the hair upright to form goose pimples, trapping an insulating layer of warm air over the body. Our muscles shiver to make extra heat.

SKIN REPAIRS

Because the dermis of the skin is a living tissue, it is able to heal itself when wounded. A wound that breaks the skin causes bleeding, and it is important to prevent this blood loss quickly. Tiny structures called platelets are present in the blood, and when they reach the wound they cause threads of tough fibrin to be produced. These trap red blood cells and eventually form a clot that seals the wound. Cells from the dermis migrate into the wound beneath the clot, which dries into a scab. The new cells reproduce, filling the wound and eventually dislodging the scab. The new skin underneath is pink and tender, but gradually takes on the same appearance as the skin around the damaged area. A scar occurs if the wound was very large or became infected, or if the scab was picked off before the wound had healed properly.

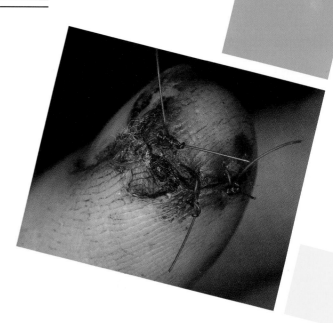

△ Deep wounds in the skin usually need stitches to hold the edges of the wound together while it heals. *(Above right)* Once collagen fibers have formed in the wound, the stitches are removed. Sometimes special stitches are used, which dissolve and do not need to be removed.

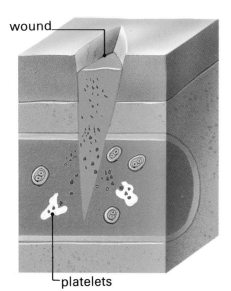

wound

platelets

△ When the skin is broken, blood seeps into the wound. Platelets in the blood help it to clot.

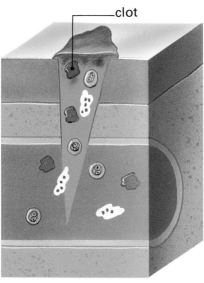

clot

△ As the clot starts to dry, it forms a scab. Skin cells around the wound reproduce themselves making new skin.

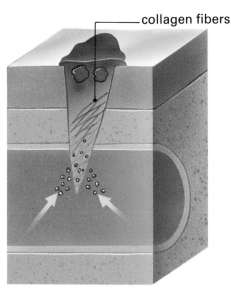

collagen fibers

△ As the scab hardens, it pulls the sides of the wound together. Collagen fibers strengthen the damaged skin.

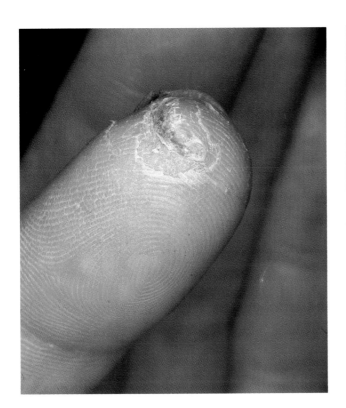

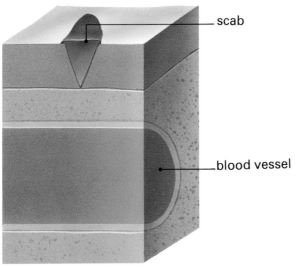

scab

blood vessel

△ When the scab falls off, the skin underneath is tender and pink but soon looks normal.

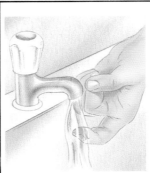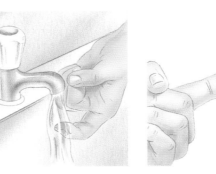

△ Minor cuts should be held under running water to remove any dirt and then bandaged.

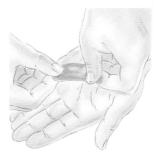

△ Blisters, if they have burst, should be cleaned gently and covered with a bandage.

▷ Splinters should be removed using sterilized tweezers. Pull the splinter out along the same path it went in.

PIMPLES

Sebaceous glands in the hair follicles produce oily sebum which helps keep the skin supple and waterproof. If not enough sebum is produced, or a person washes with powerful detergents that remove the oily sebum, the skin can become dry and scaly. If there is overproduction of sebum, the skin is very oily.

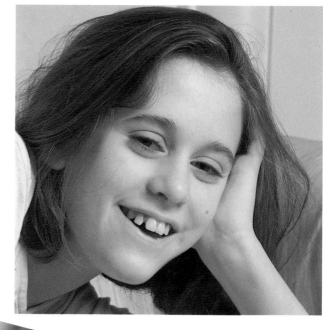

▽ Acne can result in unpleasant skin eruptions and scarring. It is common during adolescence, when the skin is oily because of extra hormone activity.

▷ Oily skin encourages pimples, and is usually associated with oily hair that needs extra washing and grooming.

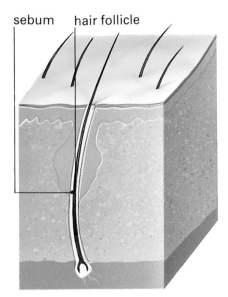

sebum hair follicle

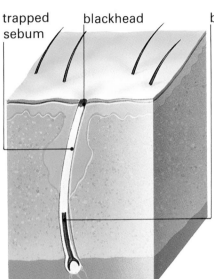

trapped   blackhead
sebum

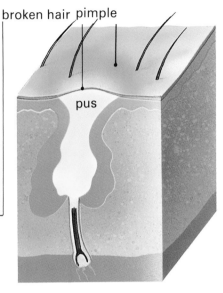

broken hair pimple

pus

△ The development of a pimple. Sebum is produced by a gland in the hair follicle. At puberty the glands often produce too much sebum, causing greasy skin.

△ Greasy skin traps dirt and dead skin cells on its surface and blocks the hair follicles. The blockage forms a hard, waxy plug which prevents new sebum escaping. The plug blackens when exposed to air, forming a blackhead.

△ Trapped sebum builds up in the follicle and is attacked by bacteria, turning it into pus. This irritates and inflames the skin around it, causing a red pimple. Sometimes the pus breaks out of the follicle, further inflaming the skin around it and forming a whitehead.

Oily skins are prone to blackheads and other skin problems. These occur when the hair follicles become blocked by a plug of sebum and dead cells from the epidermis. Exposed to air, the plugs become hard and dark, producing a blackhead. Sometimes larger amounts of sebum accumulate, producing a swelling called a whitehead. If the blockage continues, bacteria break down the trapped matter, causing inflammation and a red pimple. These pimples may continue to develop into acne pimples which contain liquid debris called pus. Acne pimples can cause permanent scarring if they are not treated effectively.

Production of too much sebum is responsible for pimples and acne, and is a result of hormone levels increasing. This happens around puberty, which is why so many teenagers suffer from pimples.

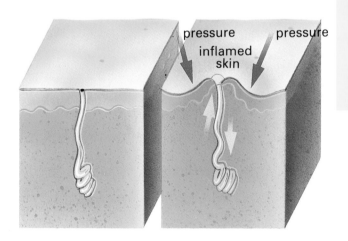

pressure   pressure
inflamed
skin

△ Squeezing a pimple does not get rid of it, as the pressure usually forces as much oil deeper into the skin as it removes.

It also further inflames surrounding skin and often allows the entry of new bacteria, making the pimple worse.

CARING FOR YOUR SKIN

The best way to care for your skin is to ensure that it is clean. The surface of your skin is covered by millions of bacteria which feed on sebum and dead cells. Normally, these bacteria are harmless but they can cause pimples and, on unwashed skin, produce body odor.

Washing regularly removes a lot of skin debris and so keeps bacteria to a minimum. To avoid body odour, it is particularly important to wash regularly beneath the arms and around the groin.

If you suffer from pimples or blackheads you should never squeeze them, because this will only spread the trapped matter into the surrounding tissue. Washing with hot, soapy water, followed by a brisk toweling to dry the skin, will unblock many of the follicles and let

◁ Washing your face with hot, soapy water removes dirt and bacteria from the skin. Frequent baths or showers remove the bacteria which cause body odor.

△ There are a huge variety of skin products on the market which claim to clear common teenage skin problems. Anti-bacterial soaps and face washes reduce the number of bacteria on the skin, and creams and lotions containing benzoyl peroxide can clear blackheads and pimples.

their contents escape. Stubborn blackheads and whiteheads can usually be cleared with a lotion containing benzoyl peroxide. But once the pimple has become inflamed, antibiotics are the only effective treatment, and these must be prescribed by the doctor.

There are many myths about the causes of pimples and acne. For example, a bad diet does not cause the condition, and neither does chocolate, or lack of fresh air and exercise. Poor hygiene may be the initial cause, but most people with acne wash more frequently than others. Oily hair flopping over the forehead is not responsible either. The direct cause of pimples and acne is production of too much sebum, and there is nothing you can do about that.

▽ There are many myths about pimples. Eating lots of fries, and chocolate, and other fatty foods does not cause pimples.

▷ Although they cannot prevent pimples from developing, exercise, fresh air and a balanced diet including fruit all help your body fight infection.

SKIN INFECTIONS

Many skin infections are caused by bacteria, fungi, or parasites, which are caught by contact with an infected person.

Boils are a very contagious bacterial infection and start in the same way as acne. But they are larger and can be very painful. Usually, the boil has a yellow head which eventually bursts. Impetigo is another bacterial infection. Usually found near the mouth, it starts as small blisters that burst and leave a yellowish encrustation. It is very important to keep boils and impetigo covered to prevent their spreading.

Athlete's foot and ringworm are caused by minute fungi growing within the skin.

Parasitic infections such as scabies, lice and nits are small organisms that live on the skin and suck blood. They are passed by contact with an infected person and can spread rapidly.

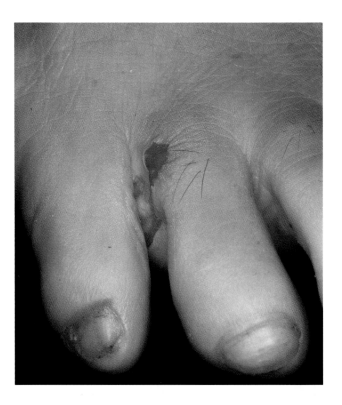

△ Athlete's foot is an infection caused by fungi growing through the skin. It usually attacks between the toes, where sweat maintains the damp atmosphere the fungus needs. Athlete's foot is often caught at swimming pools, and is very infectious.

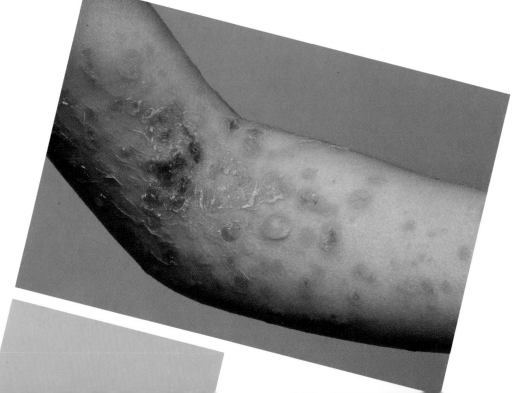

◁ Impetigo is a very infectious skin disease caused by bacteria. It causes weeping sores that need treatment with antibiotics to stop them from spreading over a large area.

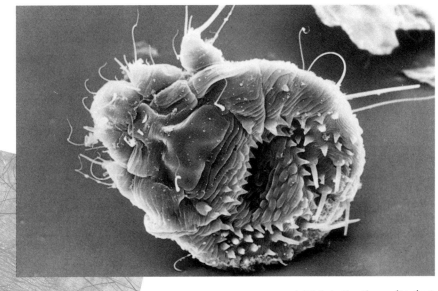

△ This is the tiny mite that causes scabies. It burrows through the skin, causing intense itching. It is easily treated using special lotions.

△ Ringworm is a fungal infection which is often caught from infected animals. The fungus grows through the skin, forming a discolored, scaly circle.

inflamed skin

▷ Boils are large, painful, red swellings which harden as they fill with pus. Eventually the boil bursts, and drains, and heals itself.

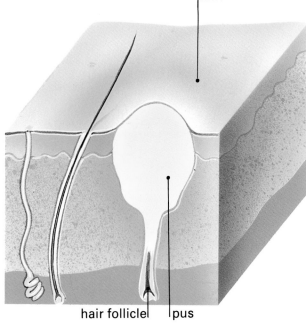

hair follicle   pus

SKIN VIRUSES

Viruses are tiny organisms that can cause disease in the skin or elsewhere in the body. It is not strictly accurate to call them organisms, because they are not alive in the usual sense. Viruses can only carry out the processes of life when they get into a living cell and 'hijack' its processes to produce more viruses. This usually kills or damages the cell. Just as it does with other disease-producing organisms, the immune system in the body attacks the invading virus, but it cannot recognize viruses hidden inside the cell. This allows viruses to lie dormant for long periods, only causing illness when the immune system is weakened.

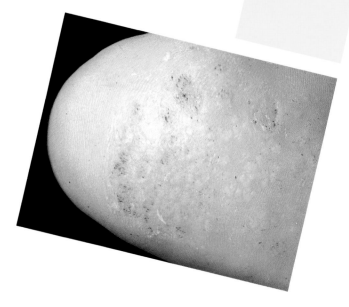

△ Verrucas are warts which grow on the soles of the feet. The pressure of body weight forces them to grow inward, causing great pain when walking. Doctors usually prescribe chemical products which cause the verrucas to shrink and eventually vanish.

◁ Verrucas are very infectious and should be covered to prevent other people from catching them. They are commonly caught at swimming pools.

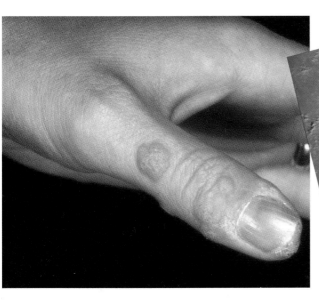

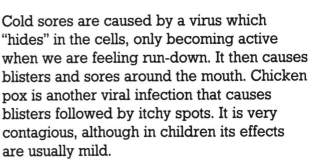

△ Warts are lumps on the skin caused by a virus infection. They are harmless but unsightly, but usually clear up without treatment.

▷ Chickenpox and shingles are caused by the same virus. This electron micrograph shows three tiny round particles of this virus.

▽ Hand and foot warts which occur near the base

of the nails need medical treatment.

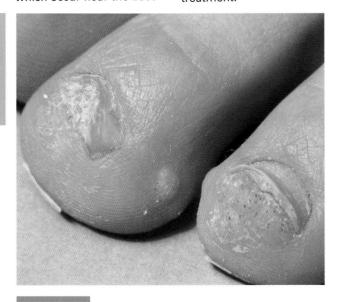

Cold sores are caused by a virus which "hides" in the cells, only becoming active when we are feeling run-down. It then causes blisters and sores around the mouth. Chicken pox is another viral infection that causes blisters followed by itchy spots. It is very contagious, although in children its effects are usually mild.

Other viruses cause warts, which are lumps on the skin caused by the virus making skin cells multiply quickly. Verrucas are similar, but they grow on the soles of the feet. Both warts and verrucas are contagious, and it is important to use good hygiene to keep them from infecting other people. Don't share towels or wash cloths with another person if you have any of these virus conditions. Verrucas are commonly caught in swimming pools, where the damp conditions around the pool allow the viruses to survive long enough to infect someone else.

ALLERGIES

The body's defense system is designed to attack unfamiliar substances. These substances that are normally produced by, or attached to, an invading organism are called antigens. They trigger the immune system, and it reacts by producing special cells and antibodies which attack the antigen and make it harmless. In some people, the system reacts in this way to an antigen, such as grass pollen, which does not cause any damage. The reaction causes hay fever.

Allergies of this type also affect the skin, causing dermatitis. The allergic reaction, caused by an antigen in contact with the skin, makes the skin red and itchy, and it may later become dry and scaly. All sorts of things can cause these reactions. Rubber used in the waist band of clothes sometimes causes skin rashes, and so do jewellery, metal watch straps and cheap earrings. Silver and gold

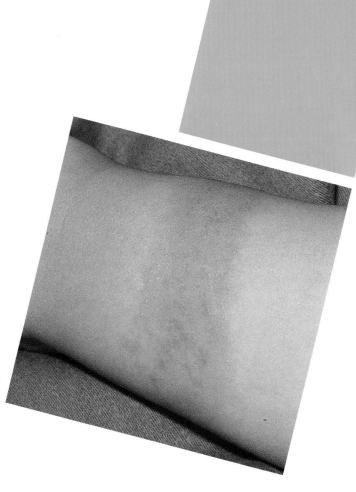

△ This contact dermatitis was caused by an allergic reaction to a plastic watch strap. The rash has exactly followed the shape of the strap. These marks often reproduce the shape of the object causing the reaction.

◁ Some forms of dermatitis can be eased by regular bathing in very salty water. The waters of the Dead Sea are particularly effective.

◁ Many people are allergic to some of the foods they eat. Strawberries and nuts are common examples. The allergic reaction often produces a red, lumpy rash called hives, or urticaria, which is very itchy.

▽ Special skin tests are used to discover which things a person is allergic to. Suspect materials are pricked into the skin, and those which cause a reaction produce a pimple or blister. Sometimes the reaction is very strong.

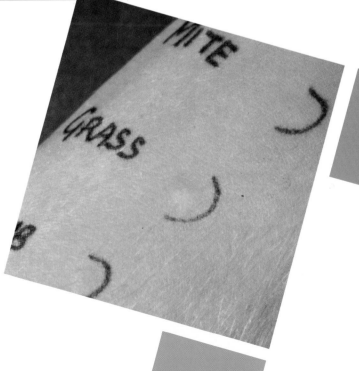

seldom cause these problems. Certain cosmetics and soaps are also likely to irritate sensitive skins.

Sometimes the allergic reaction causes urticaria, which are itchy red lumps. These can be caused by eating certain types of food, such as strawberries or shellfish, or by reacting against penicillin. Similar marks are caused by stinging insects, or jelly fish, and these usually clear up quickly.

Psoriasis is a condition in which the skin cells reproduce too fast, making thickened and flaky skin. This thickened skin occurs in unsightly patches, often on the elbows and knees. The causes of psoriasis are not understood, but it is not infectious and can be helped by medical treatment.

MARKS AND MOLES

Most people are very self-conscious about marks or blemishes on their skin. Freckles are patches of melanin, the normal skin pigment. Just as happens with ordinary suntanning, these patches of melanin darken with exposure to the sun, and the freckles become larger. They fade again when the sun is less strong, during the winter. People with lots of freckles usually appear to have pale skin, because most of their melanin coloring has been squeezed into the freckled areas.

Birthmarks are skin markings that babies may have when they are born. Some of these marks are bruises caused by the birth process, which fade quickly. Other birthmarks have a different cause. A nevus is an area of skin with many tiny blood vessels near the surface, causing a red mark. Some

△ Freckles are caused when most of the skin's melanin coloring occurs in small patches. Freckles increase in size after exposure to the sun, but the rest of the skin is pale, so people with freckles do not tan properly and often suffer from sunburn.

◁ Mikhail Gorbachev has a large portwine stain on his forehead. Some people are very distressed by these marks, and undergo cosmetic surgery to remove them. Cosmetics are also used to conceal them.

types gradually fade away, but other raised nevus marks last until the child is about three years old. Port wine stains are a permanent reddish-purple mark. Sometimes they can be removed by plastic surgery or laser treatment, or can be covered up by cosmetics.

Moles are another common type of skin blemish, and are areas of dark colored raised skin. They are harmless, unless they begin to grow suddenly, or bleed. Any changes in the appearance of a mole should be reported to a doctor immediately. Unsightly moles can be surgically removed.

Tattoos are produced by putting colored pigments into the skin with a needle. Because the coloring is deposited into the dermis, it cannot be removed except by painful surgery.

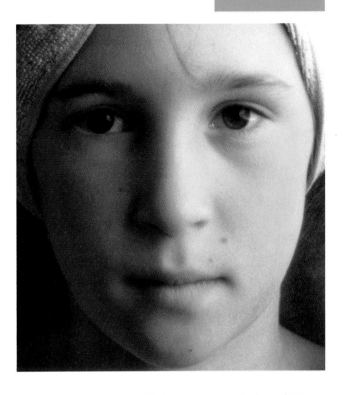

△ Moles are generally harmless skin blemishes, but can be removed if necessary.

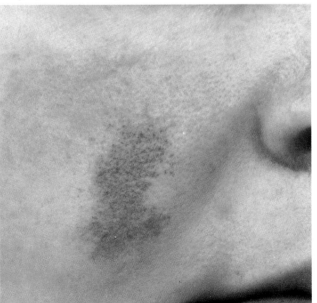

▽ This large birthmark was removed by laser surgery which destroyed some of the excess blood vessels causing the mark.

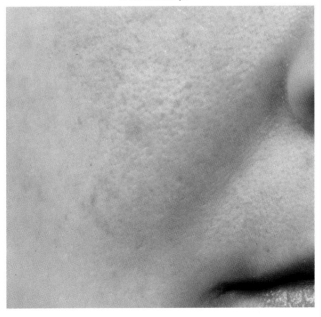

THE SKIN AND CLIMATE

Skin coloring is caused by a dark pigment called melanin. This is produced in special star-shaped cells which lie between the dermis and epidermis. When these cells are exposed to strong sunlight, they produce more granules of melanin, which spread out into the arms of the cell and into the still-living cells at the base of the epidermis. This causes the skin to darken and to filter out the harmful ultraviolet rays present in sunlight. Sunlight in moderation is good for the skin, because it produces vitamin D, but too much sun ages the skin rapidly, causes burns and blisters, and can even lead to skin cancer. In cold weather, care should be taken to protect the skin from such common problems as chilblains, frostbite and chapping.

▷ Most people like to have a suntan because it makes them look and feel good. But too much sun can damage the skin. In strong sun, it is best to protect it with a good suntan lotion or sunblock.

Chilblains are painful and are caused when extreme cold forces the blood vessels in the skin to cut off most of the blood flow from that area in an effort to conserve heat. Frostbite *(far left)* occurs when exposed parts of the body get so cold that the blood ceases to flow, and the tissues freeze.

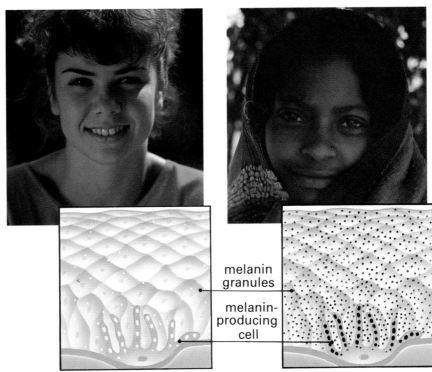

melanin
granules

melanin-
producing
cell

△ Albinos have no melanin in their skin, so they are pale pink in color.

People from cool climates need only small amounts of melanin in their skin, as the sun is not strong.

Peoples with black skin have high levels of melanin to protect them against the strong sun.

▽ Chapped lips are usually caused by exposure to very cold wind. The lips become sore and split.

▽ Dangerous skin cancers sometimes appear in people who are constantly exposed to strong sun.

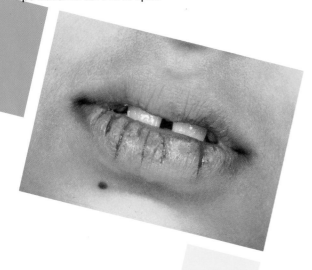

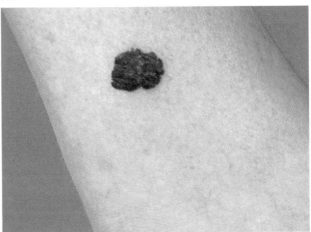

HAIR AND HAIR CARE

We have about 5 million hairs on our bodies, of which 100,000 are on the scalp. A hair is made up from a string of dead epidermal cells containing keratin. These cells overlap and give the hair its strength. Hair cells continuously divide from the base of the hair follicle. They contain pigments which give the hair its color. As we age, the amount of pigment in the cells of the hair shaft is reduced, and when pigment production stops completely, the hair looks gray or white. Each hair grows for 3 to 5 years, before being shed from the follicle.

Hair is best washed when you can see that it needs it. Washing the hair every day can remove the natural oily coating and make it appear dry. If your hair seems to need frequent washing, use a mild baby shampoo

▽ This photomicrograph of a healthy hair shows the smoothly overlapping keratin scales which give it strength and resilience. Regular brushing and avoidance of chemical treatments will keep it looking like this.

▽ In this damaged hair, the tip of the hair shaft is split. When the hair is in this condition it looks dull and matted.

△ Healthy hair is shiny and untangled, and has a slight sheen caused by its natural oils.

and follow this with a conditioner.
Conditioners help the appearance of the hair
by flattening and lubricating the scaly surface
of the hair shaft so it becomes smoother and
less likely to tangle.

Oily hair is caused by production of too much
oily sebum from the hair follicle, and is
helped by frequent washing. Dandruff is
often caused by a fungal infection of the
scalp. Regularly shampooing the hair with
medicated shampoo helps to remove dandruff.
The hair shaft is rough and becomes rougher
when it is damaged by the use of hair dyes,
hot blow driers and powerful perming
chemicals. These dry out the hair, making it
brittle, and can eventually damage the hair
shaft permanently. Damaged hair looks dull
and unattractive.

△ Nits are the egg cases
of the head louse, which
lives on the scalp. The lice
spread quickly, but can be
easily removed with a
special shampoo.

△ Hair type partly depends upon
the shape of the hair follicle it grows
from. The shape of our hair follicles
is inherited from our parents.
Straight hair grows from follicles
with a circular cross-section.

△ Wavy hair grows from hair
follicles with an oval cross-section.

△ Afro and very curly hair grows
from hair follicles with a rectangular
cross-section. Afro hair is very curly
to prevent strong sun reaching the
scalp and burning it.

NAILS AND NAIL CARE

Finger and toenails are made of keratin, the material which reinforces the skin and the hair. They grow continuously from the cuticle, so they must be trimmed regularly. Fingernails should be cut off level with the finger tips, with a curving cut, while toenails are best cut straight across.

To make the nails a better shape, it is sometimes recommended that the cuticles should be pushed back, revealing more of the nail. This is actually very bad for the nails. If pushed back far enough the root of the nail will be exposed, and this could cause infection. Any damage to the cuticle causes nail growth to be interrupted, producing a ridge or other mark on the surface of the new nail material as it emerges past the cuticle.

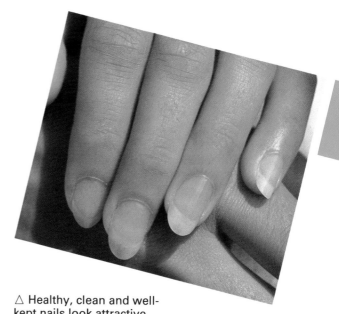

△ Healthy, clean and well-kept nails look attractive. Bitten or dirty nails look bad and can easily become infected.

▽ A hangnail should be cut off carefully. Tearing it off can be very painful and often allows bacteria and fungi to infect the nail.

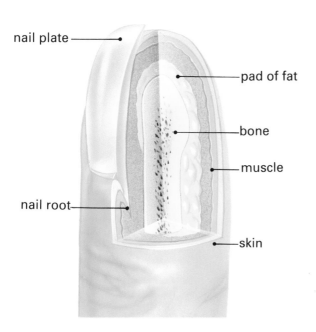

nail plate

pad of fat

bone

muscle

nail root

skin

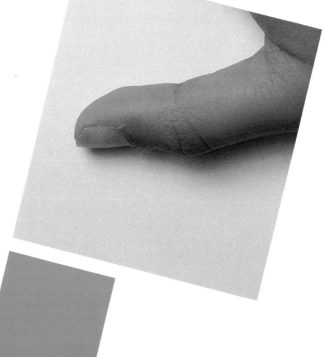

△ This is a cross-section through a fingernail. The nail grows from its root in the nail matrix and along the nail bed.

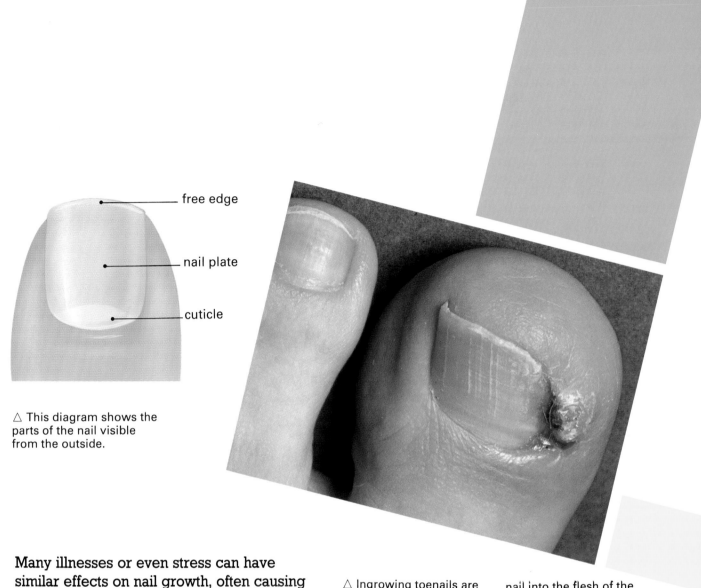

free edge

nail plate

cuticle

△ This diagram shows the parts of the nail visible from the outside.

Many illnesses or even stress can have similar effects on nail growth, often causing white flecks. Special creams can be used to keep the cuticles supple and healthy, but otherwise you should not interfere with them. Chemicals like detergent and the solvent used in nail polish remover can make the nails brittle and liable to split. Apart from making the nails look unpleasant, picking or biting the nails softens them and allows bacteria to enter around the edge of the nail. This can cause a painful infection called a whitlow, which may mean that the whole nail has to be removed.

Sometimes the nail of the big toe curves too far at the sides, digging into the flesh and causing a painful ingrowing toenail. This can usually be cleared up by a podiatrist, who will trim away the excess nail.

△ Ingrowing toenails are most common on the big toes. They are caused by wearing badly fitting shoes which squeeze the nail into the flesh of the toe, or by cutting the nails too short. Nails should be cut straight across to avoid this.

△ It is very important that nails are cut properly. Fingernails grow more quickly than toenails and should be cut more frequently. Toenails must never be cut too short as pressure from the shoes may force the nail to grow into the nail bed.

FACTS ABOUT SKIN

Skin cancers, caused by too much exposure to strong sun, are now the commonest form of cancer. If diagnosed early enough, skin cancer can usually be treated. This is a very common disease among white people living in Africa, California and Australia, where the sun is very intense.

At least 90 percent of teenagers develop acne at some time. In nearly all of them, the acne disappears by the time they leave their 'teens. Picking or scrubbing the spots can leave permanent scarring.

A "Face Lift" is a type of surgery carried out to tighten the skin and remove wrinkles on the face. This involves cutting out sections of skin, and stretching the rest of the skin tightly to flatten out wrinkles. This is a cosmetic operation, used to make a person look better, rather than an operation carried out for medical reasons. Other parts such as the eyes and neck can be treated in a similar way.

Traditionally, warts can be "charmed away" by a number of strange customs, such as rubbing them with a snail, or by giving someone else some money, in order to "sell" the warts. Actually, warts generally clear up on their own, without treatment. Sometimes, however, they spread and are unsightly, so they need medical treatment.

Many babies are born with blond hair, but this usually darkens as they get older.

Baldness in men is caused by higher than average levels of the male hormone testosterone. This form of male baldness starts as hair begins to recede from the temples and the forehead.

Fingerprints are made when skin oils are deposited on a smooth surface. The sweat glands on the finger tips are arranged in a series of raised lines, and the pattern of these lines is unique to each individual.

The Chinese knew how to carry out tattoos about 4,000 years ago. Tattooing is still practiced, but as the coloring injected under the skin is indelible, it is very difficult to remove an unwanted tattoo. Surgery to remove the affected patch of skin is often used, and laser surgery can burn away a tattoo.

A lot of babies are born with hair on their bodies. It is usually found in premature babies, and normally disappears before the birth. This long silky hair is called lanugo.

You lose an average of 30 to 60 hairs each day, but they are soon replaced by new hair growing from the follicles. It would take a long time for all your hairs to be replaced at this rate, because you have at least 100,000 hairs on your scalp.

All of the skin cells you can see on yourself are dead. The outer cells are constantly shed as they dry out and die. It takes about 27 days for a new skin cell to reach the surface of the epidermis, which is 20 cells deep.

The number of living organisms on your skin is about equal to the total number of people living in the world. Most of them are harmless bacteria and yeasts.

The skin is normally waterproof, because oily sebum on the skin sheds water quickly. If you soak for a long time in the bath, your skin becomes soft and wrinkly. This is because water eventually penetrates the dead and flattened cells in the epidermis, making them swell up and soften.

Some people will tell you that after a fright, someone's hair "turned white overnight." This cannot happen, because the hair shafts are dead keratin, and they can only change colour as they grow from the follicles.

GLOSSARY

Allergy: A condition in which the immune system of the body reacts against some harmless substance as though it was dangerous. Allergies can cause runny and bloodshot eyes, sneezing fits, and skin rashes. The metal used in cheap jewelry often causes an allergic rash, especially in pierced ears.

Antigen: Substance that may be harmless which the immune system of the body treats as being dangerous. It is often a chemical attached to a bacterium or other microbe.

Podiatrist: Someone who treats foot problems.

Clot: A mass of tough fibers and trapped red blood cells which plugs a wound so that healing can take place.

Collagen: Tough, flexible, leathery tissue in the dermis, which gives skin its strength.

Cuticle: Base of the finger or toenails from which the nail grows.

Dermis: Living layer of skin beneath the epidermis. The dermis contains hair follicles, sweat glands, blood vessels and sensory nerves.

Epidermis: The outer layer of the skin. It is about 20 cells deep, and is composed of dead and flattened cells filled with tough keratin.

Fibrin: Fibers produced when blood comes into contact with the air in a wound.

Fungus: A form of microorganism which is usually found growing harmlessly on the skin.

Gland: An organ which produces a substance which is useful to the body, such as sweat glands and sebaceous glands.

Hair follicle: Deep indentation in the skin, from which a hair grows.

Hormone: Chemical messenger carried in the blood, which regulates the operation of the organs. Adolescents have high levels of hormones in the blood, and until these are produced at the proper rate, they can cause the skin to become very oily and prone to spots.

Keratin: Tough leathery substance which is deposited in the cells of the epidermis.

Laser: Device which produces a beam of intense light, and can be used for delicate surgery.

Melanin: Colored pigment which causes the skin to darken when exposed to plenty of sunlight.

Nerves: Thread-like structures which carry nerve impulses around the body and to and from the brain. Nerves are composed of the large bundles of smaller nerve fibers.

Parasite: Organism which lives on, or at the expense of, another creature.

Pigment: A coloring substance.

Platelet: Tiny rounded body, present in huge amounts in the blood. Platelets are responsible for producing the threads of fibrin.

Puberty: The period of life during adolescence when the sexual organs are becoming fully developed.

Pus: Thick, yellowish liquid formed after an infection. It contains dead bacteria and the remains of the body's white cells which have destroyed them.

Sebum: Oily, lubricating liquid produced from glands inside the hair follicles.

PRINTED IN BELGIUM BY

proost
INTERNATIONAL BOOK PRODUCTION